A SAILMATE BOOK

HEATING AND COOLING ON BOARD

E. Lamprecht

ADLARD COLES NAUTICAL
London

This edition published in 1993 by Adlard Coles Nautical
an imprint of A & C Black (Publishers) Ltd
35 Bedford Row, London WC1R 4JH

Copyright © Klasing & Co, GmbH, Bielefeld 1993
Copyright © English Language text
Adlard Coles Nautical 1993

ISBN 0-7136-3528-2

A CIP catalogue record for this book is available from
the British Library

Translated by Robin Inches, MITI from the German
edition, *Heizen und Kühlen an Bord*.

Typeset in 11/13 Century
Printed and bound in Great Britain by
J. W. Arrowsmith Ltd, Bristol BS3 2NT

Contents

Part 1

Contents

Part 2

Acknowledgements

The author wishes to record his thanks to all those who have helped in putting together this book. In particular for tips and suggestions from experts in the fields of heating and refrigeration, and for textual and pictorial material provided by manufacturers and dealers.

PART 1

Heating on board

The season is never long enough

More and more people who go boating for fun would love to have more than just the warm summer months for engaging in their hobby, and be able to spend their free time on board for as long as possible. Of course invigorating or inclement conditions are all right for outings, but afterwards in the cabin, clammy fingers, red noses and sodden clothes may dampen the enthusiasm somewhat. If the family is to be on board as well, that may even become a decisive factor. Without a cosy warm cabin you just don't get the right atmosphere; putting this right by having heating would be so easy.

Here, as in everything else, proper planning is the secret of success. Nothing is so annoying as to discover that something won't work in practice because some point or other has been overlooked, or the proper solution wasn't known. Makeshift solutions should be totally taboo, however attractively simple they may look, because nowadays there is safe heating equipment suitable for practically any set of requirements you can think of.

The most important question is: what do we really expect from our heating installation? Do we just want to get the cabin warm quickly, or do we also want to heat water for washing, etc? Do we also want to spend nights on board, or is the boat not suitable for that? Of course, having a means for drying wet clothes would be useful too. These are just a few of the points to consider.

Some more technical questions also need to be considered: do we want to use air or water for the heating system? Which fuel should we choose? Does the heating have to be installed by the boatyard or can it be retrofitted? And if the latter, then how? Obviously the amount of heat generated must be adequate; that depends on the size of the boat and where it is going to be used, but it's dependent on other things as well. And where in the boat is there room for a heater, and how much room does the heater need? Are there safety regulations and, if so, what are they? Already it has become plain that there is a lot to be thought about: the aim of this book is to help with that process.

Safety first

Makeshift heating units are dangerous

Cold weather outside, clammy wet clothes and seat cushions with water dripping from the deckhead inside do not make a comfortable atmosphere. So in order to produce a little warmth, a paraffin lamp or portable stove may be lit down below or – an 'expert' trick this – an earthenware flowerpot is placed upside down over the open flame of the cooker and, bingo! you have heating. All of this is:

- of only limited effectiveness. 'Heaters' of this type do not counteract the increasing humidity of the air down below; on the contrary, they increase it even further.
- dangerous, indeed, deadly dangerous.

All such 'heaters' with an open flame take the oxygen necessary for combustion from the surrounding space, and discharge the products of combustion into that same space. If all hatches and portholes are shut tight and there is no effective forced ventilation, an oxygen shortage develops in the cabin and combustion becomes incomplete. Regardless of which fuel you are using, incomplete combustion produces poisonous carbon monoxide (CO) – extremely dangerous because it is odourless. What we smell may be incompletely burnt hydrocarbons; CO simply does not smell at all. But not only that: the symptoms of CO-poisoning are slight enough to be mistaken for mild seasickness. The next stage follows quickly: unconsciousness from which there would be no reawakening.

Rules for safe, efficient heating

The basic rules for a safe heater are:

1 The products of combustion must be taken outside via a gas-tight pipeline. That is an absolute *must*.
2 The air for combustion should reach the heater from outside the cabin via a gas-tight pipeline. This is very important.

This gives us 'closed-circuit combustion'. A permissible variation of this is to take the combustion air directly from the space housing the heater, such as a seat locker, engine compartment and, if there are no regulations prohibiting this, the cabin. This last is sometimes necessary in the case of stoves, or for constructional reasons. What has to be ensured in any case is that, when the heater is in use, the space housing it is adequately ventilated.

But that's not all. Portable stoves with a wick-type burner and no flue to the outside are certainly convenient; but on top of the already mentioned danger of poisoning there is also the danger of one of these devices toppling over. Maybe even on to the carpet.

3 The entire system must be securely and immovably fastened down.

4 Accessible surfaces must not get so hot that touching them could produce burns, or ignite any material making contact with the stove.

There is danger even in the fuel – though here there are differences. Diesel and paraffin are the least dangerous. Petrol heaters should be allowed on board only in exceptional circumstances; for instance if there is already a petrol engine and a petrol tank. Strict compliance with the relevant safety regulations is of course essential.

A diesel or paraffin heating system is always a better solution. It should also be noted that in certain areas (eg Sweden, Bavarian waters) the law prohibits petrol-fired heaters on board boats.

Nowadays safety regulations are strictly laid down for virtually all of a yacht's systems, not just the gas installation but the fuel supply and electrics too. Of course, compliance is very much in the skipper's interests but, despite every precaution, inadvertent mistakes can be made – especially by an amateur fitting his or her own equipment. These mistakes, whilst unlikely to hazard the boat or her crew might well cause the insurance to be invalidated. So remember two basics:

1 *ALWAYS* seek professional advice and assistance before you start.
2 Inform your insurers as soon as any additional system is installed (indeed, it makes sense to check with them beforehand as to its acceptability).

Ventilation

If you take the oxygen necessary for combustion from outside air and return the products of combustion there, you increase the safety factor. But people are also consumers of oxygen and producers of moisture. Even when resting, each one of us breathes in about half a cubic metre of air per hour and breathes out 20 litres of carbon dioxide. On top of that, each person releases 50 g of water vapour per hour. So, for that reason you must provide ventilation and dehumidification in the cabin.

The best means of doing this is a blown-outside-air heating system. If you are recirculating the heating air, other means such as partially opened hatches or portholes or, even better, continuous forced ventilation have to be used to ensure that the cabin is properly ventilated.

Choosing a system

So far we have established rules concerning safety – certain standards are indispensable.

Comfort is a different matter though. Depending on your requirements, any one of several solutions may be right for you; it all depends on how much you are willing or able to spend.

For example:

1 Do you mind fiddling about with matches and lighters, or do you want automatic ignition?
2 Do you want to heat several compartments, or are you satisfied with a little stove in the cabin?
3 Do you just want to get the cabin warm quickly for short periods of time, or do you want a heating system suitable for living on board?
4 Are you satisfied with 'control by porthole', or do you want automatic temperature control by means of sensors?
5 Are you willing to put up with the need to buy special fuel, or is the heating system to be supplied from the tank that feeds the engine?
6 How about hot water for domestic purposes?
7 Is wet clothing to be dried quickly?

None of these has anything to do with safety, just with your purse! Let's look around the marketplace, to see what's on offer. Much is available. And no wonder, since the requirements and the solutions can vary so widely.

So let's proceed systematically and subdivide what's on offer into groups – that way we can look at the whole picture more clearly.

The main criteria for this are:

1 The heating system – hot air without a blower, hot air with a blower or hot water
2 The fuel – diesel, paraffin, LPG (bottled gas)

The characteristics of hot air and hot water systems are set out in the table on page 10.

That's simplified matters somewhat. Now you should be able to make decisions.

Hot air systems are most suitable for an established heat requirement of up to about 4000 watts. Hot water heating systems generally only become viable if a much higher heat output is required.

When assessing hot water systems the following factors need to be considered:

- A water-cooled inboard engine to whose cooling circuit the heater can be connected. Engine waste heat can then be used for heating and, conversely, the cold engine can be preheated before starting
- In the case of large craft, the heating system should be incorporated at the planning stage by the yard
- Room for radiators in the boat
- Use made of the potential for heating water for domestic purposes
- One radiator with a fan drawing in air from outside, to make use of the drying effect of that air.

HOT WATER AND HOT AIR SYSTEMS

Hot water systems	Hot air systems with blower	Hot air systems without blower
Not for units below 4000 W	Units below 4000 W must be hot air (larger ones may also use hot air)	
Can be combined with existing cooling water circuit; engine waste heat can then be used	Engine waste heat cannot be utilised	Engine waste heat cannot be utilised
Domestic water heating possible	Limited potential for domestic water heating	Limited potential for domestic water heating
Water pipe dia. small: 15-30 mm	Air duct dia. large: 50-100 mm; 150 mm for very large outputs	No air ducts
Slow to heat up; control very sensitive	Quick to heat up; control not quite so sensitive, depending on appliance	Heats own compartment up quickly; control easy
Noise level low	Noise level higher; silencer required	No fan noise
Limited possibility of working with air from outside, so drying of compartment air less easy than with hot air systems	Drying of compartment air by outside air or outside/recirculated air causes no problems	Little drying effect on compartment air
Generally uses less current than same-output fan-assisted hot air system	Current consumption depends on control system. Avoid on-off control; high-low control is preferable.	Uses no current
Retrofit possible, yard-fit preferable	Retrofit possible	Retrofit very easy

If these prerequisites are not met, a system using air is recommended. For simple needs, a stove without a fan will suffice. If several compartments are to be heated, and the air in the compartments is to be dried effectively, blown air systems are the right answer. In which case, adequate control of the heat flow combined with economical use of the battery is important.

The fuel factor

The main criterion for making a choice is, first of all, what fuel is already on board. If the boat has a diesel engine you will go for a diesel heating system, and take the fuel from the existing tank.

For a small boat without an inboard engine but with LPG on board for the cooker, you might consider a gas-fired system.

Bear in mind, though, that in most cases the gas reserves will not be sufficient for both. For an hour's heating you need about 0.2 kg of gas; with that you could cook for a whole day or even two. So you will need extra reserves of gas.

Let's take another look at safety. LPG is easy to ignite and burns cleanly. However it has the unpleasant, and in boats dangerous, characteristic that being heavier than air it sinks downwards. Once 'loose' in the boat it collects in the bilges. There it needs to build up to only about 2 per cent in the air to form a flammable mixture, and then even the smallest spark can cause an explosion. A gas-fired heating system, including the bottle storage and pipelines, must therefore be especially installed to comply with BS 5428 and carefully maintained and operated.

For heat flows up to about 3 kW, paraffin heating systems are an option. However, they also require an additional fuel container and an additional fuelling operation to acquire the paraffin!

11

Other factors

Power consumption

Combustion-air blowers, an efficient hot air blower or, in the case of hot water systems, a circulating pump – they all need power. For heating systems up to 5000 watt heat flow, you have to reckon on a power consumption of 20 to 50 watt. With an on-board voltage of 12 V that means a current consumption of 1.7 to 4 amps. As well as the starter battery, a second battery is therefore essential.

Controllability of the heat flow

Hot water systems offer the greatest convenience, since the thermostat valves on the radiators allow precise adjustment to provide the desired heat, just as with domestic central heating. Similar adjustment is available on the small oil stoves without a fan for the burner: again, just as with domestic oil stoves. In the case of blown hot air systems you have to watch it. If control is by an 'on-off' thermostat this creates no problems with LPG systems; gas ignites readily and so re-ignition after the 'off' phase requires only a little power. Diesel and paraffin however are not so easy to ignite and systems firing those with 'on-off' control need a lot of current. That isn't a problem in harbour and when on shore power, but when running on the battery, diesel and paraffin systems should be controllable between 'low', possibly 'medium', and 'high' to keep the current consumption within bounds.

Air throughflow of hot air systems

The next important point concerns the quantity of air which the heating system fan is able to deliver against the resistance of the air ducts and inlet/outlet fittings. The longer the ducts, and the smaller their bore, the greater this resistance. But of course there would be no point in having a heating system if this is incapable of conveying the heat to where it is wanted. So the fan must be appropriately powered and this again means using more current. Checking up on equipment consumption is a simple process.

When comparing different products with differing current consumption, you must therefore find out about blower output.

Noise

Blown systems are obviously not as quiet as hot water systems or stoves. But substantial noise reduction can be achieved by installing the system outside the cabin, and fitting silencers to combustion-air, exhaust, outside and hot air ducts.

Modern hot air and hot water systems

To conclude this general survey, before dealing specifically with matters such as heat requirements, location, air ducting, water circulation, piping for combustion air and waste gas, fuel supply, etc, here are a few examples of modern boat heating systems.

A simple heating stove using diesel

This type of heating system is the most simple method of generating heat safely on board. The diesel fuel runs from the tank through the control unit into the cup burner, on the lower surface of which it forms a thin film which burns evenly. The stove can put up with rolling, but not with a persistent angle of heel which causes the oil to run to one side. The tank is installed at least 20 cm above the control unit.

The waste gas is taken outside via the flue and chimney, through the deck/roof of the steering position. Ignition and control is the same as for domestic oil stoves.

Adequate ventilation of the compartment housing the stove is of vital importance.

Choosing a system

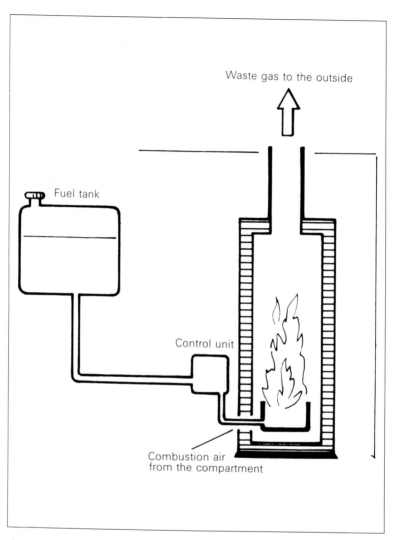

Waste gas to the outside

Fuel tank

Control unit

Combustion air
from the compartment

A simple diesel stove

Paraffin heater for
installation in the
cabin

Fully automatic, blown hot air heating systems

Fuel: diesel, paraffin, LPG
Heating system: air, water

Depending on basic design and size, these systems are intended
for installation either in the cabin or outside it in stowage space
or in the engine compartment. Installation in the cabin elimi-
nates hot air ducting but the equipment takes up space in the
living area.

   Installation outside the cabin means that the heat is transported to where it is required in the boat via appropriate air
ducts or water pipes. This is the most convenient way of providing heating on board. The following description of a diesel
hot air system illustrates the operating principle.

In the diesel hot air unit shown below, a fan draws air from outside via the air duct and conveys it to the combustion chamber. There it is mixed with the fuel, supplied in precisely the right quantity by the metering equipment (in this case a pump), and the mixture ignited by an ignition device (here a glow plug). After a short interval a stable flame is established which burns in the heat exchanger and transfers heat through the latter's walls to the air flowing past outside. The waste gas generated, as with every combustion process, is taken out into the open by a gastight duct.

Both heating air and location compartment are thus hermetically separated from the products of combustion (waste gas). The air reaches the spaces to be heated via the hot air ducts driven by a second blower fitted in the heater. Once the desired room temperature is reached, a rotary switch can be turned to

Diesel hot air unit; heat flow 3200/1600 watts

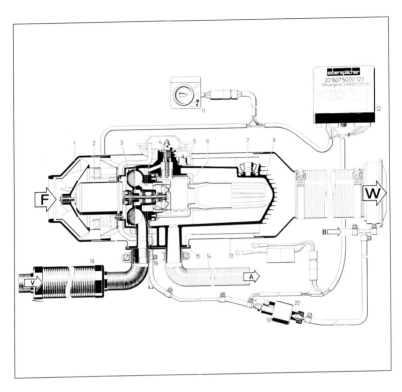

Diesel hot air unit

1 *Outside air blower impeller*
2 *Electric motor*
3 *Combustion air fan impeller*
4 *Glow plug*
5 *Overheating cut-out*
6 *Combustion chamber*
7 *Thermal switch*
8 *Heat exchanger*
11 *Master switch*
12 *Control unit*
13 *Outer casing*
14 *Waste gas pipe*

15 *Connecting flange*
16 *Fuel supply connection*
18 *Combustion air silencer*
19 *Fuel metering pump*
20 *Pot-shaped strainer built into fuel metering pump*

F = Outside air
W = Hot air
V = Combustion air from outside
A = Waste gas
B = Fuel

1 *Outside air induction*
2 *Combustion air*
   induction

3 *Waste gas duct*
4 *Hot air outlet*
5 *Changeover flap*
6 *Heater*
7 *Electronic control unit*
8 *Container for*
   condensation
9 *Fuel metering pump*
10 *Fuel supply connection*
   on diesel tank
11 *Silencer*

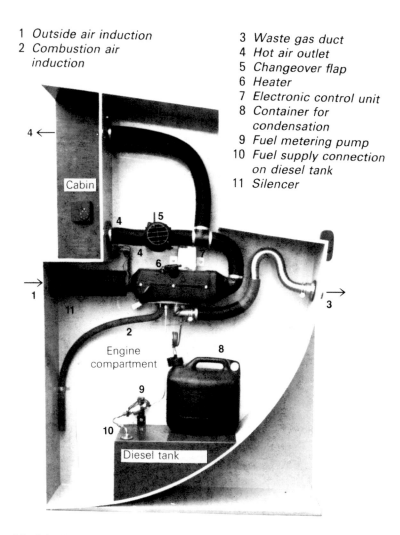

Model of a hot air heating system installation

This arrangement is only an example; it can easily be adjusted to take account of individual requirements. For instance, the changeover flap could be fitted in the intake line to permit changeover from outside air to internal circulation or a mixture of the two; the silencer could be fitted in the hot air duct, etc.

low or else a room thermostat does this automatically. What about safety?

Obviously no piece of technical equipment can always be guaranteed to function perfectly. If there is a breakdown it is important that this should not create a dangerous situation. The equipment discussed has built-in safety devices which automatically shut the heater down in the event of failure to ignite, flame failure while running, or overheating. Which all makes for a safe piece of equipment.

Diesel hot water system; heat flow 7000/1750 W

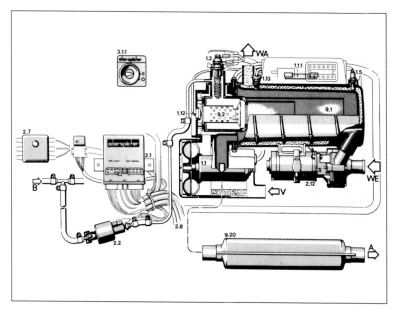

This diesel-fired heater is started by means of a rotary switch.
Everything else happens automatically.

1.1	Burner motor	9.20	Silencer for waste gas
1.1.1	Rheostat resistance for part load	2.2	Fuel metering pump
1.2	Glow plug	2.7	Fuse box
1.5	Overheating cut-out	2.8	Cable harness
1.12	Flame sensor	2.12	Water pump
1.13	Temperature sensor		
3.1.1	Master switch	WE = Water inlet	
9.1	Heat switch	WA = Water outlet	
9.2	Combustion chamber	V = Combustion air	
		B = Fuel supply	
		A = Waste gas	

Hot water heating systems

The operating principle of a hot water system is almost the same as that for the hot air system. In place of the hot air fan wheel there is a water pump driving the water heated in the heat exchanger, and this is transported to the radiators in the cabins via the pipe system.

This system also contains the same safety equipment for failure to ignite, flame failure while running, or overheating. The heat flow can be varied between full and $\frac{1}{4}$ output, depending on the heat requirement of the radiators.

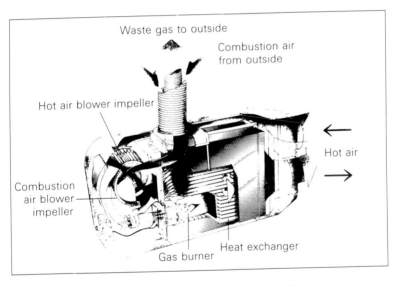

LPG-fired hot air equipment; heat flow 3700/1850 W

The appliance comprises a burner for LPG, a light alloy heat exchanger, the hot air blower for transporting the hot air and the usual safety devices. Waste gas and combustion air are conveyed to/from the outside in concentric ducts. The appliance can be operated at full and half output levels. Control by thermostat is possible.

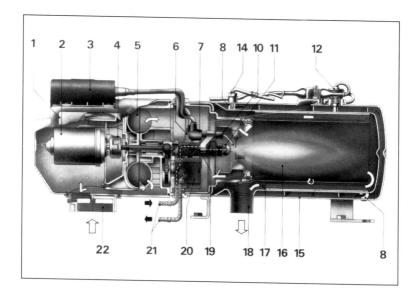

◀ Diesel hot water system; heat flow 11,600 watts

The equipment illustrated is suitable for large motor yachts. Many of the components we already know about: heat exchanger, combustion air blower, fuel transport and metering apparatus, temperature control unit and thermal cut-out to protect against overheating. In this system, the water pump is installed separately.

1 *Control unit*	12 *Thermal cut-out*
2 *Motor*	14 *Temperature sensor*
3 *Ignition coil*	15 *Heat exchanger*
4 *Coupling*	16 *Combustion chamber*
5 *Combustion air blower*	17 *Swirler*
6 *Solenoid valve*	18 *Waste gas outlet*
7 *Plug cap*	19 *Flame failure monitor*
8 *Water pipe stubs*	20 *Fuel pump*
10 *Ignition electrodes*	21 *Fuel lines*
11 *Atomiser*	22 *Combustion air inlet with control*

Combined cook-and-heat

The idea of using the cooking equipment for heating also is nothing new for us – remember the flower pot over the gas flame?

Don't even entertain the idea!

Mind you, the basic concept does have its attraction, only it would need to be safe. And safe cook-and-heat combinations do indeed exist. Here is an option for small boats.

The basic equipment is a two-ring paraffin or diesel cooker, with a sealed-off flame heating the rings. Combustion air comes from the cabin; waste gas is taken outside through a gastight duct. That meets one important safety requirement. If there is effective cabin ventilation, there can be no reservations about taking the combustion air from inside the cabin. It is vital, though, that the cabin is adequately ventilated when the cooking equipment is in use.

The beauty of the system, though, is that the cooker has a

lid housing a fan. During cooking this lid is raised; so heating is not possible whilst you are cooking. But when you finish cooking, you lower the lid and now the fan draws the compartment air over the rings, where it is heated.

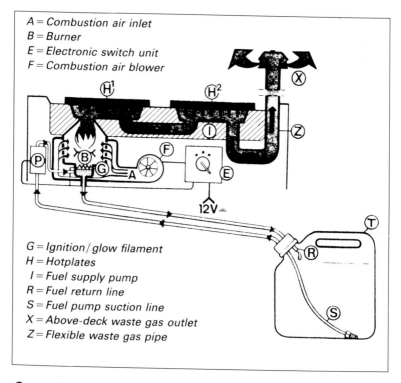

A = Combustion air inlet
B = Burner
E = Electronic switch unit
F = Combustion air blower

G = Ignition / glow filament
H = Hotplates
I = Fuel supply pump
R = Fuel return line
S = Fuel pump suction line
X = Above-deck waste gas outlet
Z = Flexible waste gas pipe

Operating principle of the cook-and-heat combination

Start-up begins when you switch on the electronic control unit (E). The fuel supply pump (P) starts pumping paraffin from the tank (T) to the burner (B). The combustion air blower (F) feeds air to the burner. The glow filament (G) glows for two minutes and thus ensures ignition of the burner flame.

The hot products of combustion are led through the hot plates (H1 and H2), after which they pass via a flexible waste gas pipe and the above-deck outlet into the open.

A cut-out interrupts the fuel supply if the unit should overheat.

Heat requirement – equipment size

First of all, what is this 'heat flow' that features in all the catalogues? Heat flow (previously called heating power) is the term for the amount of heat the heating equipment can produce. The heat flow is measured in watts and is part of the data the manufacturers state in their advertisements and catalogues. To be able to select the right heating equipment all you need to do then is – establish the heat requirement of your boat. 'All', did you say? Because the establishment of the heat requirement can involve the most laborious calculations. The size of the compartments, the bulkhead material, the area of window glass, all must be taken into account; where the boat is to be sailed, and the length of the working season, also need to be considered.

For very large vessels, in some of which several heating installations are fitted, that is certainly worthwhile – but it's best to get experts to consider for individual cases. Most cases can be dealt with much more simply: boat length is the criterion.

Since the range of heating equipment on offer can't be graded that finely for output, the choice is limited. In a marginal situation, you would in any case have to opt for the more powerful equipment and see to it that effective control of the heat flow is possible.

For that reason, there should be enough information in the three examples that follow to allow you to calculate the requirement for your own boat.

1 Sailing/motor boat up to about 8 m length
  Hot air equipment, 1800 watts
2 Sailing/motor yacht 8 to 11 m long
  Hot air or hot water equipment, 3000 to 5000 watts
3 Sailing/motor yacht 11 to 14 m long
  Hot air or hot water equipment, 7000 watts or 2×3000 watts.

To provide the required heat, it will often be better to install several small heating units instead of one larger unit. For instance, for a very large yacht with a total requirement of 14,000 watts, possible combinations might be:

2×7000 watt hot air units or
2×7000 watt hot water units or
1×7000 watt hot air unit $+ 1 \times 7000$ hot water unit

Installation of the heating system

Examples and tips from practical experience

Every heating equipment system does, of course, have a set of installation instructions, in which the manufacturer provides advice on any points needing special attention. But there are some general points which apply in every case. Let's start with where the equipment should be located, and examine the running of the ducting for the hot air units.

Depending on the design of your boat, the possibilities are:

1 The cabin
2 The seat locker
3 Other stowages
4 The engine compartment

Heating stoves should as far as possible be sited in the coldest place in the cabin, eg by the companionway, but care must be taken to avoid injury to the crew in severe conditions. A crash bar to prevent a crew member coming into accidental contact with any hot surface is essential. A drip tray underneath the stove is strongly recommended, to catch any oil that might run out. Such a tray is mandatory for commercial vessels.

Other designs are intended for fixing to a bulkhead.

Heating appliances with blowers for installation in the cabin

Anything fitted in the cabin takes up space there. In addition, the hot air from these units enters the compartment to be heated high up; low down would be better. Thus we come to the equipment that can be located outside the cabin, and take the hot air via flexible air ducting to the outlets inside the cabin.

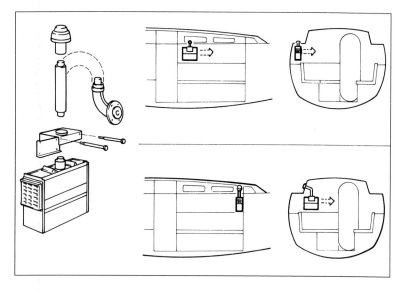

Since no air ducting is required, these appliances can simply be installed by suspending them from the fitting carrying the waste gas pipe through the deck, or from the bulkhead.

Blown air heating systems with air ducts

Possible locations are: seat locker, other stowages, engine compartment. Three ways of ducting the air are possible:

1 Outside air operation – the air to be heated is drawn from outside.
2 Closed-circuit operation – the air to be heated is drawn from the compartments to be heated.
3 Mixed operation – the air to be heated is taken partly from outside, partly from the compartments to be heated. The fresh air/circulating air ratio can be adjusted by means of a changeover flap in the suction line.

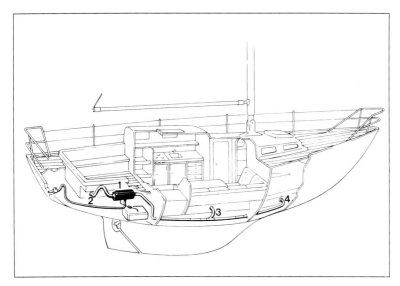

Hot air heating system (diesel) with blower in an 8 m sailing yacht; location: seat locker

The heating air is drawn in from outside (2) (outside air operation), heated up by the heater (1) and distributed to the cabin and the berth. The hot air emerges from the outlets (3, 4) of which the one in the forward berth (4) can be shut off.

7000 watt installation in the engine compartment of a motor yacht

1 *Heating appliance*
2 *Outside air ducting with silencer*
3 *Hot air ducting with silencer*
4 *Waste gas pipe*

A system using outside air is the preferred option, because this continuously renews the compartment air and, at the same time, removes moisture. To ensure a proper flow-through, this has to be combined with an effective waste air outlet (permanent vent, opened hatch, etc). In summer this system can be used for cabin ventilation.

The closed-circuit operation does have the advantage that it works faster. But moisture extraction is less effective than when using outside air.

The ideal solution, where this is possible, is mixed operation which combines the two. In all installations, the correct relationship must be maintained between heating air duct diameter and duct length. Too small a diameter/too great a length causes the equipment to overheat and shut down automatically. Similarly, if there are two outlets only one of them may be closable, and

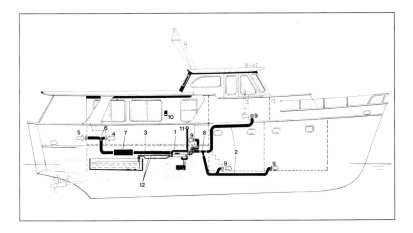

7000 watt hot air heating system in a motor yacht

Location: the engine compartment.
The heating air is either drawn in from outside or recirculated;
the changeover flap (6) can also be set to give a mixture. Heated
compartments are the saloon, helm position and two sleeping
cabins. To avoid noise from the engine compartment being carried
through to the living spaces via the air ducts, silencers are built
into these. The use of silencers is very important where the
equipment is located in the engine compartment.
   Where the hot air ducting has several branches, as is the case
here, the total outlet-opening area must be at least 150 per cent
of the heater outlet cross-sectional area.

1 *Heating appliance*
2 *Hot air ducting*
3 *Outside / recirculated*
  air ducting
4 *Recirculated air inlet*
5 *Outside air inlet*
6 *Changeover flap*
  outside / recirculated
  air

7 *Silencer*
8 *Hot air duct branch*
  piece
9 *Hot air outlets*
10 *Thermostat*
11 *Waste gas pipe*
13 *Fuel pipe*

the flow area remaining must not be less than the required minimum.

Furthermore, care must be taken to ensure that the blower is powerful enough to transport the required amount of air, otherwise the heater will overheat, and be switched off by the automatic shut-off.

All manufacturers provide information concerning minimum diameter and maximum length of the heating-air ducting.

Water for domestic use, heating with a hot air system

In our survey of the special characteristics of hot air and hot water heating equipment we mentioned that hot air equipment offered limited potential for heating water for domestic use. However, where the boat engine has dual-circuit cooling, it is then possible to use engine waste heat in the boiler for heating the water. But what if the engine isn't running or cannot produce enough heat? You don't need to make do without hot water; the boiler just has to be designed to use heating-air for heating the water.

The illustration opposite shows what such an installation might look like.

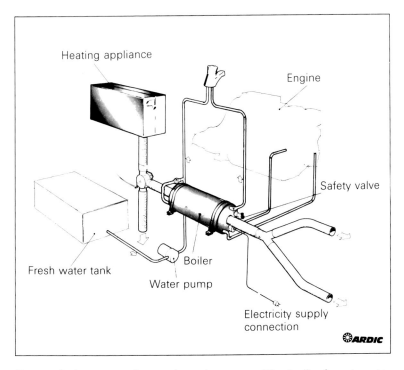

Heating appliance

Engine

Safety valve

Fresh water tank

Boiler

Water pump

Electricity supply
connection

ARDIC

Domestic hot water from a hot air system. The boiler is set up to
receive water heated by the engine, the hot air heating, and
electricity from the shore connection.

Hot water systems: heater location, pipe runs, radiators and domestic water heating

Let us briefly re-state the special features of hot water heating:

Advantages: even heat distribution, stepless regulation, low noise level. The system may be combined with the existing water circuit, in which case engine waste heat may also be used for heating and conversely the engine preheated. Domestic water heating practicable. Diameter of pipes conveying heat substantially smaller than that of air ducts. 'Comfort' as with household central heating.

Disadvantages: radiators take up cabin space. Slow to heat up. Little drying effect on compartment air, so additional radiators with blowers drawing in outside air required.

Hot water system heaters are usually installed in the engine compartment, where the domestic water heater (boiler) is also located. Furthermore, necessary safety devices (expansion vessel, safety valve, pressure gauge, float vent, drain/filling cock) can be accommodated here.

The design and installation of a hot water heating system calls for a lot of expertise.

A few key points: single- or double-line system? What sort of radiators, and where should they be located? Ensuring that the pipeline bore is commensurate with the radiator output, fitting a circulating pump with the correct capacity.

Since the propulsion engine is also included in the water circuit, cooling water and heating system thermostats have to be compatible etcetera, etcetera. Truly a job only for the experts.

All the same, you should acquire a general picture of how the whole thing works, so that at least you are able to take part intelligently in a discussion! The illustration opposite summarises the minimum you need to know.

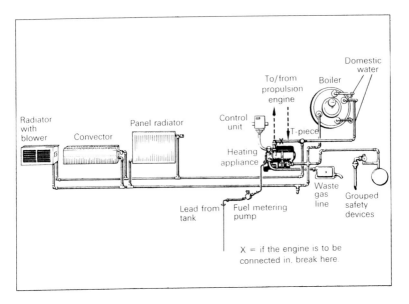

The hot water heating system. The hot water flows from the heating appliance to the T-piece. This distributes it to the boiler and to the radiators; it is then collected in the return line and flows back to the appliance.

Fuel supply arrangements, electrical control equipment and the 'safety group' complete the installation.

A mixing tap in the domestic water line allows cold water to be mixed-in as desired.

The arrows with broken lines show the connections to/from the engine, which can be included in the heating circuit.

The schematic diagram below shows one of these installations in a motor boat with dual-circuit cooling. This allows the engine to be included in the heating circuit, to use engine waste heat for heating and the heating system to preheat the engine. With direct or single-circuit cooling, where 'raw water' flows directly through the engine cooling passages, that is not possible.

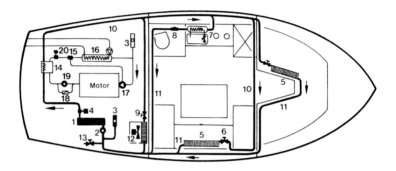

Hot water heating system in a motor yacht. It is a double-line system, ie the supply line (10) and return line (11) are separate.

1 Heating appliance
2 Appliance-associated circulating pump
3 Expansion vessel
4 Control thermostat and temperature limiter
5 Radiator
6 Control valve
7 Domestic water heating
8 Flow rate regulator
9 Regulating valve or slider
10 Supply line
11 Return line
12 Radiator with blower (eg for helming position)
13 Filling and drain cock
14 Heat exchanger
15 Engine coolant thermostat
16 Engine radiator with pump
17 Engine circulating pump
18 Non-return valve (only when preheating engine)
19 Circulating pump (only when preheating engine)
20 Thermostat for cutting out circulating pump (2) (to prevent engine coolant temperature being too low)

What does this installation provide?

1 Cabin and steering position heating using the water heater
2 The same using engine waste heat
3 Domestic water heating in the boiler
4 Engine preheating using the water heater

At the heart of the system is the water heater (1). There the water is heated then flows through the supply line (10) to, first of all, the water heat exchanger (14).

If the engine is to be preheated, heat is transferred to the engine cooling water circuit. Conversely, when the engine is running, waste heat from it can at this stage, be fed into the heating circuit.

Next the supply pipeline goes to the boiler/domestic-water heater (7), radiators (5) and blower-equipped radiator (12). The return line (11) collects the now cooled water and leads it back to the system circulating pump (2). The boiler here is in a bypass line: the boiler line serves also as a bypass to allow water to circulate even if all the radiator valves are shut.

You can see clearly that with a double-line system and radiators on different sides of the boat you get long pipe runs across the boat. In that respect the single-line system, where the radiators are arranged along the main line and only the boiler has a line of its own, would be better. However, it is then necessary to ensure that the radiators at the beginning of the line, which get the hottest water, have special fittings so that the flow through is less than that through those at the end of the line.

And what types of radiator should be considered?

Sectional radiators are generally speaking not suitable for boats; they take up too much room and are too heavy unless they are of light alloy. Most popular are panel radiators, convectors, and heat exchangers with blowers.

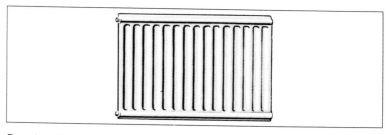

Panel radiator: available in various lengths and heights, as well as in single, double or triple form, the latter with convection surfaces in-between.

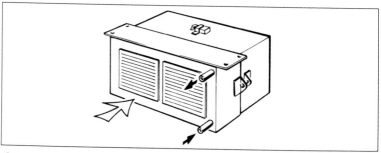

On a heat-output basis, radiators with blowers need the least space. Also they permit operation with outside air for drying the compartment.

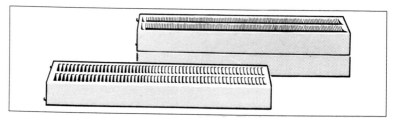

Convectors are finned tubes. These also are available in various lengths, heights and widths. To function effectively they have to be fitted in a case with air inlet slots at the bottom and outlet slots at the top.

The pipe system

Just as in a hot air system the blower has to be powerful enough to convey an adequate amount of heating-air through the ducting to the outlets, so in hot water systems the piping has to be so dimensioned that the amount of water circulating does not drop below the permissible minimum. That is a calculation for the expert.

Since water expands when heated, there must be an expansion vessel to accommodate the extra volume arising.

This must always be a sealed pressure vessel, because of the danger of any oxygen entering the system: oxygen causes corrosion, particularly if the system comprises several materials, eg steel or aluminium for the radiators and copper for the pipes. The closed-circuit installation initially has all the air carefully expelled; fresh oxygen cannot subsequently gain access. (Unless the system is drained before every winter and refilled with water before the new season.)

So, even in boats that are not used all the year round, leave the water in the heating system and add anti-freeze.

To complete the closed-circuit installation there is a safety valve, pressure gauge and float vent, combined in one group for expediency.

Run of waste gas and combustion air ducting

One of the most important safety regulations is: waste gas must be taken out into the open via a gastight duct! How to achieve that is looked at next. Plus, how the air necessary for combustion is conveyed to the heating appliance.

Let's begin with the simplest, the stove. Stoves take the combustion air from the compartment in which they are situated, so effective ventilation of the cabin must be assured. The waste gas from heaters of this type must always be conveyed above deck level. And care must be taken to see that the outlet hood is unobstructed and not affected by wind deflected downwards by the superstructure. In an extreme case, that could extinguish the stove flame. On sailing boats this hood is removed when under sail, and the aperture closed.

Run of waste gas and combustion air ducting for blower-equipped heaters

Depending on the design and manufacturer, combustion air and waste gas ducting can be up to 5 m long. This allows you to get to the side of the boat, to the transom or above deck level.

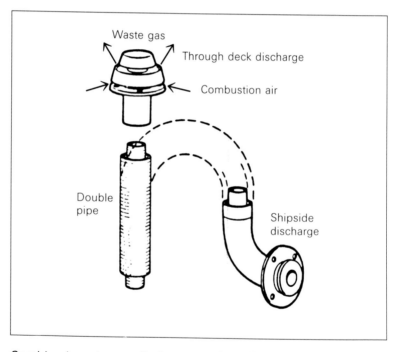

Combined waste gas discharger and combustion air supply duct

In every case, that of course means taking the pipes out through the side of the ship or through the deck. If there is an engine, that will have an exhaust pipe. Wouldn't it be possible to lead the heating system waste gas duct into the engine exhaust pipe? That would save one hole through the side! Sorry, that is not allowed. With the engine running, the pressure pattern would be disturbed to such an extent that the heater wouldn't burn properly.

Depending on the manufacturer, there are various solutions to the problem of how to run the waste gas ducting and the air ducting. In some designs the waste gas discharge and combustion air inlet pipes are combined: a concentric double pipe takes the air in and carries the waste gas out. At the same time, this arrangement insulates the waste gas pipe thermally.

Other designs have the waste gas and air ducts separate; in these cases also, the waste gas duct needs insulating. That's not just to provide external protection, it also prevents the gas cooling down too far and an excessive amount of condensation forming. It is not possible to avoid that totally, so unless the duct can be run with a continuous downward slope to its outlet, a drain from its lowest point to a collecting vessel should be fitted.

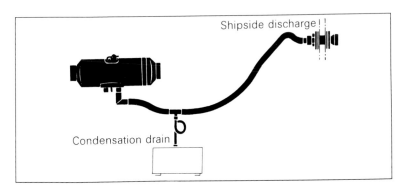

Waste gas discharge line with condensation drainage

Close to where they are taken out through the boat's side, air and waste gas ducts have a 'swan-neck' length to prevent water that has slopped in from running onwards to the heater.

If there are no official regulations prohibiting this, the combustion air can also be taken from well-ventilated stowages (seat locker), the engine compartment or the cabin – if their ventilation is guaranteed when the heating is on.

In the case of the engine compartment, you must of course be sure that even when the engine is running a low pressure area will not be generated, eg by the engine fan.

To conclude discussion of this subject, here is a sketch of an installation in a seat locker.

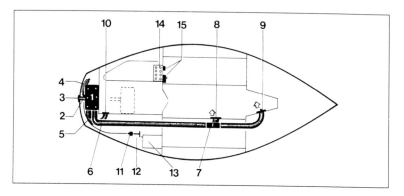

Installation right aft makes for an extremely short waste gas pipe which here can slope downwards. The combustion air is drawn from the seat locker, via a silencer.

1 *Heating appliance*
2 *Waste gas pipe*
3 *Shipside discharge*
4 *Induction line silencer*
5 *Flexible hose (outside air induction)*
6 *Flexible hose (heating air)*
7 *Heating air distributor*

8 *Outlet fitting, swivelable*
9 *Adjustable louvre*
10 *Inlet protection grid*
11 *Fuel metering pump*
12 *T-piece*
13 *Fuel tank*
14 *Batteries*
15 *Master switch or room thermostat*

The fuel supply system

Let's say it again: only in exceptional cases should petrol be used as fuel. More acceptable fuels are: diesel, paraffin and LPG.

Points to bear in mind in this connection are: storage of the fuel (tank, extra fuel containers, gas bottles), transport of the fuel from storage to heater, fuel pipe material and safety measures.

Diesel and paraffin

Let's start with the systems using diesel. There, storage presents no problems whatever. Because, unless it's a stove that you have installed, the container is already on board: the tank for the engine. Either the heating system is connected separately to the tank or a tapping is taken from the fuel pipe to the engine. Transport of the fuel from tank to heater requires a pump which can double up as the metering device.

As is already the case in certain waters, regulations are coming into force as to the types of piping permitted for all permanently charged fuel lines: these must be if softened copper, stainless steel, aluminium alloy or (in the case of diesel only) of mild steel. Furthermore, they must be run clear of the exhaust system(s) and also of any heating unit itself.

If however a diesel stove or a paraffin heating system is to be installed, an additional fuel container is needed. For the stove, the engine tank can't be used because the stove fuel supply is by gravity, not via a pump, and paraffin is a special fuel which obviously has to have its own container. The diagrams shown on page 44 show examples of how such extra containers can be installed.

Installation of the heating system

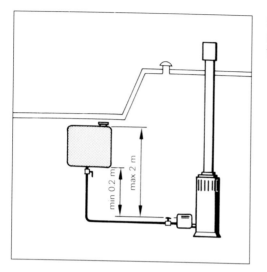

Installation of a supplementary tank for a diesel stove

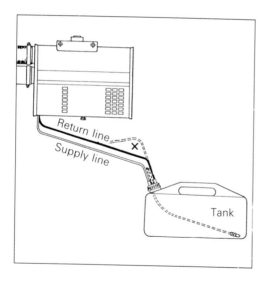

Installation of a paraffin heating system

Liquefied petroleum gas (LPG)

Now let's look at LPG. On board boats LPG has to be handled with the greatest of care: safety regulations are stipulated by Lloyd's and also by such organisations as the British Waterways and the National Rivers Authority, all of whom produce detailed guidelines and installation specifications for yachts and boats.

The storage and type of gas bottles, equipment and piping must all conform to BS 5482 part 3 – although at the time of going to press, some amendments to conform with new EEC directives are possible. (The small portable stoves and heaters with a small gas cartridge screwed directly into the appliance

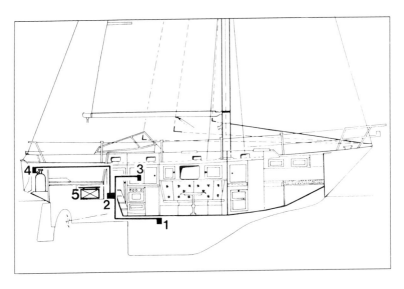

Gas-sensing system:

1 Sensor
2 Sensor switchbox
3 User position
4 Remote operated valve
5 Battery

are not necessarily prohibited in all cases but both appliance and cartridge must be stowed in an appropriate site on deck or in a cockpit locker when not in use.)

After the initial testing by the installer, a test certificate is made out confirming that the system is in proper working order. Routine confirmatory tests should then be carried out every two years and after any repairs.

Just to make quite sure everything is safe, installation of a gas detection system is recommended. This permits opening or shutting-off of the gas line at the bottle stowage by pressing a button at the appliance site; additionally the sensor automatically gives the shut-off signal should unburnt gas start to collect where the user equipment is located. To that end the sensor is located at the lowest point of the cabin, for instance underneath the cooker, immediately above the floor. However it should not make contact with water, so should not be fitted in the bilges.

This automatic gas lock-out equipment provides additional safety, but it is not a licence for incorrect installation.

Electricity supply

Obviously you need not waste time thinking about the electricity supply to your heating system if it doesn't need any power. That is an undeniable advantage of stoves. But they are inefficient at distributing heat to more than one compartment and there is little drying effect, as we have already discovered. A clear picture of our heating requirements and the power supply must be matched to these. When drawing up the electrical energy balance (Watt inventory) for your boat you must, therefore, take account of the heating system.

For example: you might want to install a blown hot air system with a heat flow (heating power) of 3000/1500 watts. As with any other equipment, you need to start by taking the operating current from the manufacturer's catalogue.

Example 1

Let's say the starting current (2 min) is 5.0 amps.
Running on 'high' takes 1.5 amps while running on 'low' takes 0.9 amps.

That's the easier part of the job!

Determining the time in use is more difficult. Factors such as whether you're under way or in harbour, what geographical region you're in, how many people there are on board and, of course, the climate outside – all these play a part. But you need to work out the time in use for your energy balance, because the current requirement of the heating system in amps multiplied by the time in use in hours gives the battery load in ampere hours (ah).

Let's follow the example of every technician when faced with an awkward problem to calculate and start with some assumptions. First let us assume that our on-board network has to be supplied by the battery for 24 hours without recharging. Then we make the following assumptions on the amount of time the heating system is in use (a = amps; h = hours; ah = amp hours):

Start-up requires 5 a × 2 min. = 5 a × 0.03 h = 0.17 ah
The system then runs for 2 h on 'high' = 2 h × 1.5 a   = 3.00 ah
6 h on 'low' = 6 h × 0.9 a   = 5.40 ah
1 h on 'high' = 1 h × 1.5 a   = 1.50 ah
Then switched off for 9 h = 9 h × 0 a   = 0   ah
then again 2 h on 'high' = 2 h × 1.5 a   = 3.00 ah
4 h on 'low' = 4 h × 0.9 a   = 3.60 ah
So for a 24 h period the load is   = 16.50 ah
Plus 2 × 0.17 ah for starting   = 0.34 ah
Total ah   16.84   = 17.00 ah

So when drawing up the energy balance for your boat, you have to enter a battery load of 17 ah – for this heating system and for the assumed length of time in use.

Example 2

Hot air appliance with a heat flow (heat output) of 3,200/1600 watts, ie about the same size as the first example. The starting current (2 min) needed is 20.0 a. The operating current on 'high' is 3.75 a while on 'low' it is 2.0 a.

Based on the same times in use and operating sequence we get:

Start up requires 20 a × 2 min	= 20 a × 0.03 h	= 0.70 ah
2 h on 'high'	= 2 h × 3.75 a	= 7.50 ah
6 h on 'low'	= 6 h × 2.0 a	= 12.00 ah
1 h on 'high'	= 1 h × 3.75 a	= 3.75 ah
9 h switched off		= 0.00 ah
Start 20 a × 0.03 h		= 0.70 ah
2 h on 'high'	= 2 h × 3.75 a	= 7.50 ah
4 h on 'low'	= 4 h × 2.0 a	= 8.00 ah
Total ah		40.15 ah

For the same length of time in use, this appliance demands more than twice the battery capacity of the first example. Why is there such a difference?

Let's begin with the starting current. Example 1 is a paraffin appliance, example 2 operates on diesel. Diesel needs more energy to ignite it than paraffin. However, since the high current load lasts only a short time (about 2 min) and only occurs when starting (note operating sequence) this is not really a problem as the sample calculations show.

The mystery of the higher operating current is solved if we look at the air volume, the issuing temperature of the hot air, and the permissible length of hot air ducting and its diameter or rather cross-sectional area.

The amount of heat the heating-air is able to transport is proportional to the air volume multiplied by its temperature, ie assuming the same heat flow that means small quantity, higher temperature; large volume, lower temperature.

Now in practice the issuing temperature should not be too high, or it will feel unpleasant; so more air is better. Furthermore a high flow rate is important for a good drying effect. The values for the two assumed heating appliances, on 'high' setting and heating-air intake temperature 20°C in each case, are:

Example 1: Paraffin appliance, air quantity about 53 kg/h.
Example 2: Diesel appliance, air quantity about 140 kg/h.

Now all is made clear. The diesel appliance has a much more powerful blower than the paraffin one, and delivers at least two-and-a-half times the amount of air.

With the appropriate battery capacity you can install heating with a high air throughput and make use of the associated advantages and comforts. If you don't need the high blower power, a smaller battery will suffice. How to get the battery capacity right for your boat is a different matter.

Wiring the installation

The wiring diagrams differ from type to type; the manufacturers will include these with the installation instructions. The following however is universally applicable: all electric leads have a resistance opposing the flow of current. The thinner they are, the greater that resistance. Thus they also consume electric power, reducing the voltage at the appliance correspondingly. So if there is a long run of lead between battery and heating appliance, don't stint on the thickness of the lead cross-section – especially in the case of appliances requiring a lot of current.

A guide (supply and return lines added together):

Up to 5 m: 4 sq mm cross-section
5 m up to 8 m: 6 sq mm cross-section
8 m up to 14 m: 10 sq mm cross-section.

Thermostatic control

As already mentioned, liquid fuel appliances should always be of the type with control settings for full and partial heat flow, not just an 'on' and 'off' switch – otherwise the high starting current would be needed after every 'off' phase.

Don't mount the room thermostat in the vicinity of hot air outlets, or where it may be exposed to draughts (near doors, hatches) or it won't operate efficiently.

There are also electronically controlled heating appliances which have the temperature sensor inside the appliance, the temperature being preselected at the circuit closer. These don't require any additional thermostat.

The installation of a diesel hot air heating system

The first thing that everyone should ask themselves is: would I trust myself to do this sort of work? In fact, installation of hot air heating systems by a skilled owner, with practical DIY experience and prior expert advice, is not too difficult.

More difficult is the installation of hot water systems; it is better to leave this to the boatyard or the specialist heating system companies. As well as the necessary expertise, they have the proper equipment and tools for the job.

On safety grounds, installation of gas-fired systems is always a job for the expert.

We are now going to have a look at the installation of a 3200/1600 watt diesel hot air system by a boatyard in a 10.6 m sailing boat.

The heater is installed under the chart table and is controlled by a room thermostat sited near the navigation instruments.

A wooden block is adhesive-bonded to the hull; the heating appliance mounting is bolted to this. Hot air ducts are run to the outlets in the saloon, the forward compartment and the after cabin.

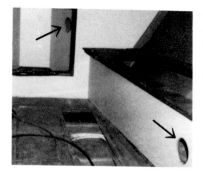

Holes are cut for the air outlets in the saloon and the forward compartment.

The heating appliance is pre-assembled with mounting bracket, ▶ heating and combustion air intake silencers, waste gas silencer and insulated waste gas pipe, electronic control unit and wiring. It is bolted to the wooden block adhesive-bonded to the hull. Heating air and waste gas ducting, fuel line and wiring are secured.

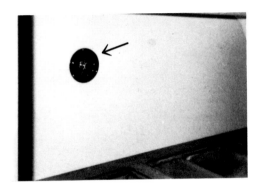

Left and centre below: Outlets in the forward compartment and the after cabin have fittings that can be shut off.

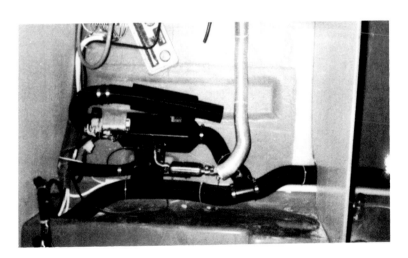

The installation of a diesel hot air heating system

The waste gas stack on the side deck is removable; the deck aperture sealable by means of a stopper in case of extreme heel. That, of course, means no heating.

Fuel line connection to the tank in the seat locker. Built into the line is the metering pump which meters the fuel as it is pumped.

The finished installation of the heating appliance under the chart table.

The room thermostat for operating the heating and selecting the temperature, built into the navigation corner.

PART 2

Refrigeration and air-conditioning on board

Refrigerating foodstuffs

Now you've achieved a cosy atmosphere below deck, even when it's really cold outside, let us turn to a second important subject. It is of course during the warm, sunny days that life on the water is the most enjoyable. In a heatwave, the crew always have the option of a quick dip to cool off.

But what about butter, milk, meat and the indispensable drinks? You can't just tow them along behind in a shopping net. Modern technology must come to our aid: after all, at home, fridges and freezers have long been standard equipment.

The simplest solution to the problem of keeping foodstuffs cold would, surely, be to fit a standard fridge in the boat. Nearly right, but refrigeration on board calls for special attention to a few points which rarely feature in domestic situations. These are:

1 Power requirement
2 Space requirement
3 Weight
4 Attitude dependence (ie heeling)

There is, of course, the matter of cost but that's not peculiar to boats. Also when cruising in really hot weather, perhaps in tropical climates, you need to be able to keep, not only the food cool, but also you and the crew, so you may consider air-conditioning the cabin(s).

This part of the book looks at what is on offer and gives some guidelines when choosing cooling systems. Once again the choice is bewildering, so we'll tackle it systematically. We'll deal separately with foodstuff refrigeration and compartment air-conditioning, and start with the simplest version of the former – insulated boxes, which are well known and good value.

With the aid of cold packs that have been deep-frozen in the domestic freezer, insulated boxes keep pre-cooled food and drink cool for a considerable length of time. An acceptable solution for the Sunday afternoon outing. But, fortunately, you can do better than that.

Peltier-effect cold boxes

Thanks to an effect which the Frenchman Peltier discovered in the nineteenth century, it is possible to convert electric current directly into cold (or heat if you reverse the direction of the current). This is achieved in so-called Peltier elements. If these are built into thermally insulated boxes, it is possible to heat or cool the contents, depending on the direction in which the current flows.

There are lots of cooling and heating boxes fitted with Peltier elements on the market. In all of them, the current consumption at 12 V nominal voltage lies between 2.5 and 4 amps (depending on size). And, due to the pretty low efficiency of the Peltier elements, they take a relatively long time to reach their maximum efficiency.

It's best to use them only for pre-cooled food and drink and if possible to pack in some deep-frozen cold packs as well, to reinforce the cooling process.

Some examples of Peltier cold boxes currently on the market. A special characteristic of Peltier boxes is that by simply changing over a switch the contents can, if desired, be heated instead of cooled. But at great cost in electrical energy, which is always scarce on board!

Oscillating-compressor cold boxes

This appliance can only cool, but does so more efficiently than a cold box. Cold boxes with oscillating compressors with a current consumption of 3.5 to 5 amps attain 5°C in about one-third of the time taken by Peltier boxes, but are in fact able to cool down to about -18°C. In their case it is the high starting currents which apply an undue load to the battery, because the compressor starts and stops frequently for short runs.

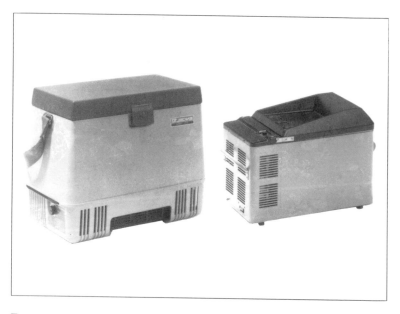

Two examples of oscillating-compressor cold boxes currently on the market. An important factor for both Peltier and oscillating-compressor systems is the unimpeded removal of the heat extracted from the goods being cooled. For built-in appliances, a fan which speeds up heat removal is very useful.

For more demanding cooling tasks, something more is needed – and the energy supply problem has to be solved. It is worth aiming, therefore, to build up a reserve of cold when there is enough power available – from a shore supply or because the engine is running – to be able to use it for cooling when power is short (for instance when under sail or anchored overnight in a bay).

How is cold generated?

'Generate cold' isn't the correct term, according to physicists! What you in fact do is take heat away from the body you wish to cool. And how do you do this? Two simple experiments which anyone can perform demonstrate the principle.

1 If you pour a highly volatile liquid (eg alcohol) over your hand, after a short time you will experience a sensation of cold. This is because the liquid evaporates, ie turns into vapour, and takes the energy necessary (heat of vaporisation) from what is nearest – your hand.
2 Liquid in a container wrapped in a damp cloth stays below the ambient temperature; especially if you keep re-wetting the cloth. Here again, the heat of vaporisation is taken from the contents of the container.

Were it possible to construct a closed circuit in which the evaporating liquid – its vapour – was captured and turned back into liquid, one could let it evaporate again and wouldn't need to keep on re-wetting. In every refrigerator, freezer, and piece of cold-generating equipment that is exactly what happens.

However, evaporation is a pretty slow business. For a liquid to vaporize more rapidly it has to boil, ie be hotter than its boiling point. But the basic principle of boiling does not differ from that of evaporation – the liquid turns into vapour, only a lot faster of course.

To make an effective circuit, a device is necessary which turns the coolant vapour back into a liquid. To this end, two laws of physics are utilised:

1 Every liquid during evaporation absorbs heat, in our case taken from the goods being cooled, and releases this again when reverting from the vaporised to the liquid state.
2 The temperature at which a liquid boils (boiling point) and condenses is pressure-dependent. The higher the pressure, the higher also the boiling point.

For instance at 1 bar (normal ambient pressure) water boils at 100°C. At 2 bar, however, it does not boil until 120°C. So we get steam/water vapour at 1.0 bar and it can be converted into water by raising the pressure to 2 bar. The heat it takes up during evaporation is released again in the process.

However, water is not suitable as a freezing agent because its boiling point is too high. Fortunately there are liquids which boil at substantially lower temperatures. One of these is freon 12; its boiling point at ambient pressure is around -30°C. This is what is normally used nowadays in refrigerating appliances.

The principle of refrigeration using a compressor

Every compressor-based cooling system has an evaporator, a compressor, a condenser and a power control.

That is all that is necessary for keeping food cold. To parallel the refrigerator at home, all you need do is to fit the evaporator into a cold chest. This sort of system is available either ready-installed in the boat or for DIY installation.

Depending on how well the chest is insulated, the compressor will run a longer or shorter time to bring the goods to be cooled down to the desired temperature. The compressor then switches off automatically. The cooled goods eventually start to warm up again, since even the best insulation does not provide complete screening from external conditions. Finally, the compressor is switched on again and the cycle is re-started. But is there any way of storing the cold?

The eutectic plate

Just as evaporation, ie conversion from the liquid into the gaseous state, requires heat which can be extracted from the goods to be cooled, so heat is also needed to change a material's state from solid to liquid. This is called latent heat of fusion, and can

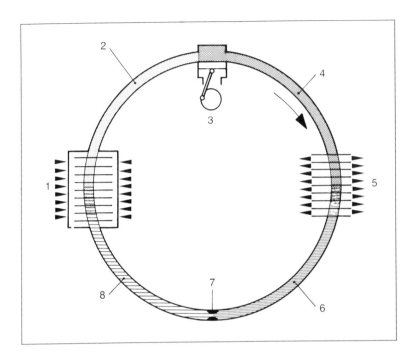

This is what the complete refrigerant circuit looks like:

1 *Evaporator. The latent heat of evaporation is extracted from the goods to be cooled in the form of vapour*
2 *Low-pressure vapour*
3 *Compressor: raises vapour pressure*
4 *High-pressure vapour*
5 *Condenser. The refrigerant condenses; the heat taken up during evaporation is given up to the outside*
6 *High-pressure liquid*
7 *Throttling device: lowers liquid pressure*
8 *Low-pressure liquid*

be made use of. All you need do to produce a reservoir of cold is, immerse the evaporator in a liquid which solidifies at a (relatively) very low temperature.

This is how it works:

1 The contents of the reservoir are liquid.
2 The compressor runs, the refrigerant extracts latent heat of fusion from the storage liquid; the storage liquid solidifies.
3 The compressor stops. The contents of the reservoir melt slowly, taking up the heat in the food to be cooled and any heat that penetrates the chest insulation.

What this means is that, even while the compressor is stopped, the temperature of the eutectic plate does not rise until the whole of its contents have melted. This substantially increases the length of time for which the compressor is stopped.

That has brought us pretty close to the ideal on-board refrigerating arrangements, and we can now leave theory behind and turn to practical installations.

Refrigeration system with compressor, for DIY installation

Commercially available compressor refrigeration system

Apart from the size of the eutectic plate, the most important distinguishing feature is the way the compressor is driven. Refrigeration systems are available with:

1 Electrically driven compressors
2 The compressor driven mechanically from the engine
3 The compressors, one driven electrically, the other from the engine

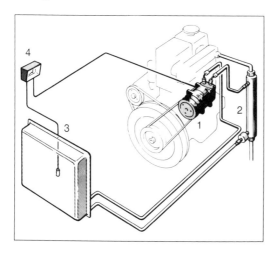

Compressor system mechanically driven from the engine

1 *Engine drive compressor*
2 *Condenser*
3 *Eutectic plate (evaporator)*
4 *Control unit*

Commercially available compressor refrigeration system

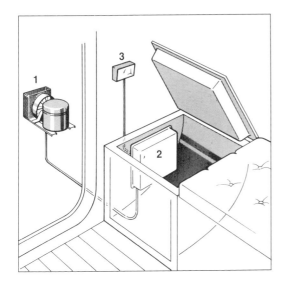

Left and below:
Electrically driven
refrigeration
system with
compressor

1 Compressor
  with blower-
  cooled
  condenser
2 Eutectic plate
  (evaporator)
3 Control unit

Commercially available compressor refrigeration system

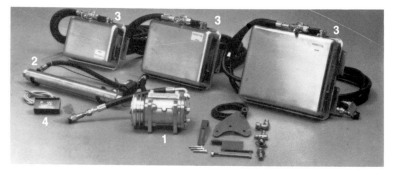

1 *Compressor*
  with magnetic
  clutch
2 *Condenser*
  (sea water
  cooled)

3 *Eutectic plate*
  (evaporator) for
  70, 120 and 250
  litres
4 *Control unit*

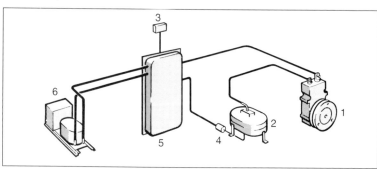

System with two compressors

1 *Engine-driven compressor*
2 *Water-cooled condenser*
3 *Thermostat*
4 *Drier-filter*
5 *Eutectic plate*
6 *Electrically driven compressor with air-cooled condenser*

This arrangement makes it possible to operate the refrigeration system without having to start the engine – for instance during a lengthy stay in harbour.

Electronics in refrigeration

The biggest problem for every refrigeration task on board is the satisfactory supply of electric power. Even if you have a generously scaled second battery, you still have to manage its capacity. The eutectic plate is already one important step in that direction, but there are few appliances that are not capable of improvement. In this instance, it's modern electronics which produce increased convenience. Here is an example: a 150 litre capacity cold chest with eutectic plate, electrically driven fridge compressor, engine-driven generator, 12 V/150 ah general use battery, shore connection with charger.

Without electronic control the fridge compressor runs and charges the eutectic plate, regardless of the state of charge of the battery or of whether the engine and generator are running or the shore connection is made. Once the thermostatically set or permanently programmed-in temperature is reached, the compressor switches off.

If the eutectic plate is still thawing out, however, the compressor will not run even if generator- or shore-supplied power is available. Once that phase is completed the compressor will be switched on again, regardless of the battery's state of charge. If circumstances combine unfavourably, the battery can discharge.

Electronics make use of the fact that the on-board voltage is a bit higher (above 12.8 V) when the generator is running, or there is a supply from shore, than when the system is supplied by the battery. Then it is less than 12.6 V.

First of all there is low-voltage protection: below about 11 V the electrical compressor is stopped whatever the situation. Complete discharge of the battery is prevented; it has to be charged.

For refrigerating purposes there are now several ways of making use of times when power is plentiful and of covering the periods of power shortage most effectively.

One system has the switching temperatures permanently programmed: if the on-board voltage is more than 12.8 V, compressor and blower are in business. The eutectic plate is cooled to -15°C; then the compressor is stopped. At -8°C it is started again automatically.

If the voltage is less than 12.5 V the compressor, in 'economy mode', is run only to keep the plate between -6 and -1°C.

Other systems enable the cold chest temperatures to be freely selectable. When the engine is running or there is a short supply, the eutectic plate is 'charged' as described above. Once that is achieved, the electronics change over to support mode. If then at some time there is no longer an external power supply, the compressor can be stopped manually by pressing a button; failing that, the unit carries on running until the voltage has dropped to 11.3 V before being stopped automatically.

The plate then remains in the 'discharging' state, making no demand on the battery, until the on-board voltage is raised above 12.8 V by running the generator or by shore supply. Then the electronics automatically switch back to charging the plate.

Detailed information about which plant is the most suitable for any given case is available from the manufacturers of refrigerating systems.

Absorption-type refrigerator installations

There is a second possible way of circulating the refrigerant: the absorption principle. It dispenses with the compressor, ie it has no moving parts.

An absorption-type system has the advantage that it is absolutely silent and can use LPG as well as electricity as the

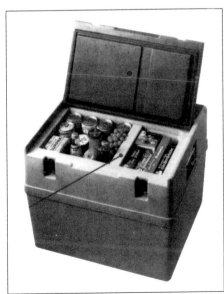

Absorption-type cold box with freezer compartment

power source. Its disadvantage for on-board use is that it is more attitude-sensitive (ie heeling) than a compressor system. It is suitable only for ordinary refrigerators or cold chests, not for eutectic-plate chests.

If you decide in favour of an absorption-type refrigerator or cold chest, you have to establish how far it can tilt for safe operation, and what constraints there are in installing this type of system.

Another important criterion is the power requirement (whether from electric current or LPG).

How does the absorption-type system operate?

There is no change to the principle that heat has to be abstracted from the goods to be cooled and conveyed somewhere else. A refrigerant is also required whose boiling point at normal pressure lies below the temperature to which you want the goods to be cooled, but which at higher pressure liquefies at normal temperature and so can discharge outside the heat taken from the goods to be cooled. Finally, everything still has to happen within a closed circuit.

Now we come to the difference between this and the compressor system. We said there is no compressor, yet the pressure of the evaporated refrigerant has to be raised. Ammonia, the refrigerant in this case, has the characteristic of being soluble in water at low temperature, but being driven off at a higher temperature, leaving the water behind.

This is how it works: in the evaporator (1) liquid ammonia evaporates because the temperature of the goods to be cooled is above the low-pressure boiling point of the refrigerant. The latent heat of evaporation is taken from the goods to be cooled and is now vapour. In the absorber (2) ammonia vapour at low temperature and pressure dissolves in water. In the boiler (3) the ammonia is driven off again from the water; ammonia

vapour at high pressure is produced. The water is returned to
the absorber. The boiler is heated by electricity or LPG. In the
condenser (4) the ammonia vapour condenses because the condenser temperature lies below ammonia's high-pressure boiling
point. The heat extracted in the evaporator from the goods to
be cooled is released outwards.

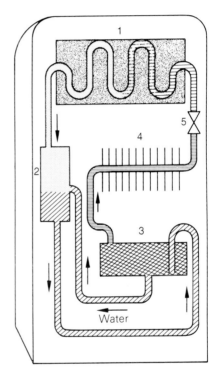

Schematic diagram of an
absorption-type unit

1 *Evaporator*
2 *Absorber*
3 *Boiler*
4 *Condenser (liquefier)*
5 *Throttling device:*
  lowers pressure of liquid
  ammonia

Constructing a chest fridge/freezer

If a cold chest is not already included in your boat's equipment, with a little manual dexterity you can build one yourself. Generally speaking a chest is always to be preferred to an upright unit, unless special steps are taken in the case of the latter. The chest has two advantages: first the cold air stays in the bottom when contents are removed or added, secondly a chest can be matched relatively easily to the shape of the boat and the equipment in it.

First of all, of course, a suitable place for installation has to be found. Shown opposite and on page 80 are some examples to start you thinking.

Since only the eutectic plate, which works totally silently, is inside the chest even the bunk can be utilised for installation. Compressor and condenser are installed separately, in a place where the heat from the latter can be dispersed easily (eg in the engine compartment). The chest itself should not be near the engine or the heating system, otherwise it will need extra thermal insulation.

Installing a cold chest in the galley...

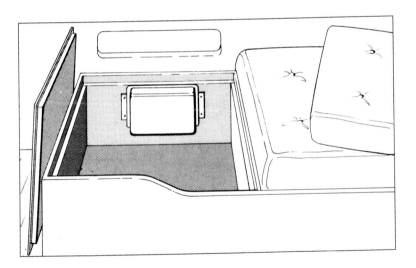

...underneath the bunk

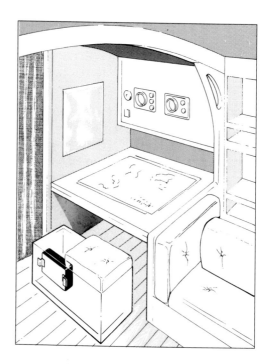

...under the chart table

Materials

High-quality insulation is a must. The most suitable for chests of around 50 litres capacity is 50 mm thick transversely bonded vinyl cell plastic sandwich (density 30 kg/m). Divinylcell, Bony-cell and similar materials will do equally well.

This material comprises a 1 mm thick polyester-film on the inside, a 50 mm thick insulating core in the middle and a 1 mm thick layer of plastic on the outside, which means that there is little risk of cracks developing and moisture seeping in.

For very small chests (up to 25 litres) 30 mm thick material will do; chests of 75 to 100 litres require material even thicker than 50 mm.

This is how you go about building a chest fridge/freezer yourself:

1 Cut cardboard templates for the parts required.
2 Cut out the parts (padsaw) cutting towards the inside of the laminate to get a clean edge on the inside.
3 Prepare reinforcing/fixing strips for the baseplate and glue them to the underside of the plate using silicon glue.
4 Glue baseplate and sidewalls together using silicon glue. Start with the baseplate. Surfaces to be joined must be clean, grease-free and dry.

   Glued joints are safe to handle after about an hour but take 24 hours to harden fully.
5 If desired, cut a 10-12 mm dia. condensation drain hole in the baseplate, glue in a drain pipe stub, fit a hose onto it and, if possible, lead this into the bilges or a sump.

   If no drain is provided, the condensation which collects has to be removed with a sponge from time to time.
6 Drill holes in the sidewalls for the eutectic-plate instantaneous couplings. Mount the plate as high up as possible.
7 Fit an internal partition (Perspex). This way you get a freezer compartment next to the eutectic plate plus a fridge compartment. At the bottom leave a gap between the separate compartments.
8 Cut an opening for the lid into the top cover plate; make the lid according to the sketch either as a trap-door with hinges or as a loose insert. Tight sealing of the lid is very important to prevent warm air leaking into the chest. For that reason the lid must have a rubber sealing strip (window seal).
9 Glue on cover plate.
10 Install the chest in the boat.

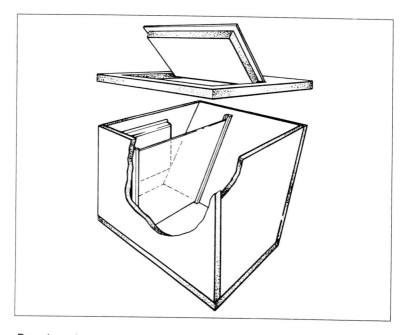

Drawing showing a home-made chest refrigerator with freezer compartment next to the eutectic plate.

Chest refrigerator installed in the galley next to the cooker. The location is convenient, but not ideal because of the heat generated by the cooker.

A different solution: the cold chest in the sofa bench.

Constructing a chest fridge/freezer

Refrigerating system with an electrically driven compressor, and cold chest with eutectic plate, in an 8 m sailing boat.

Above: The cold chest and eutectic plate next to the sink.

Below: Compressor unit and condenser installed underneath the sink and the crockery storage below this.

Installing a refrigerator in a crockery locker in a 7.6 m sailing boat

There isn't always sufficient, or suitable, space to house an extra cold chest if the one provided is too small. One possibility is to do without the crockery locker and convert this into a fridge – as has been done in this example.

The crockery locker is lined all-round with 40 mm thick Styropor, or preferably polyurethane, and secured with double-sided adhesive tape or casein glue. A specially made box is fitted into the space.

This insert is given about 4 mm clearance at the sides, top

The crockery locker converted into a refrigerator closed by a door hinged at the bottom.

A look into the home-made refrigerator. At the top, the eutectic plate; at the bottom, a vegetable tray.

and back so that it can be pushed in easily. Plastic foam is used to fill the gaps between the box and the inside of the locker.

The next job is the door. This can of course be hinged-on, but it is simpler to seat it in a groove at the bottom and hold it with a bolt at the top.

For effective insulation, all joints must be tight so that warm air can't leak in. Seal any cracks with adhesive tape.

Mounting the eutectic plate, compressor, and connecting refrigerant pipes and thermostat is the final task.

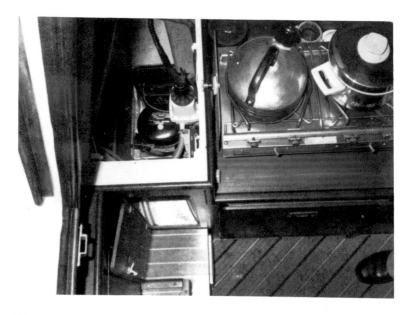

Compressor and condenser have been installed in the space next to the refrigerator. This space must be adequately ventilated.

Let's summarise again the possibilities for refrigerating food-stuffs on board:

1 *Movable*: cold boxes with cold packs, Peltier refrigerating boxes, compressor refrigerating boxes with built-in electri-

cally driven compressor, with or without eutectic plate, absorption-type boxes powered by electricity or LPG.

2 *Installed*: refrigerating chests with eutectic plate with electrically driven compressor, with mechanically driven compressor (propulsion engine), with two compressors (one electrically, one mechanically driven).

3 *Refrigerators*: compressor refrigerators, compressor refrigerators with electronically controlled eutectic plate, absorption-type refrigerators.

What you decide to install depends on a multitude of factors: where the boat is sailed, average trip duration, boat size, boat type (sail or motor), crew number, type of engine, energy sources available (gas, electricity), electrical capability (generator, charger) – and lastly even the price may come into it. So, don't do your planning without expert advice.

Energy-saving tips when refrigerating

1 Always try to pre-cool foodstuffs ashore.
2 Before starting to fill the chest, sort out the goods to be stored and lay them out ready nearby. That way you avoid opening the chest for too long.
3 Keep the chest tidy. The division between freezer and fridge compartment is clear, but it would make little sense to put at the bottom what you are going to need first, so that you have to re-pack everything when you take that out.
4 Lastly, try to avoid the most frequently committed sin: waiting for inspiration as to what's on the menu until you have the chest lid (even worse – the refrigerator door) open and the contents in front of you. That can waste a lot of power.
5 To keep an eye on the temperature of the contents, without having to open the chest, an electronic distant-reading thermometer is very useful.

Air-conditioning the cabin

The next step might be to air-condition the cabin. In northern latitudes that is not a matter of great importance; heating is much more necessary. But in the Mediterranean area, and even more so in the Caribbean, cooling is worth thinking about. What can you do about excessive heat below deck? There are several possibilities.

- Put up a canvas or synthetic-fibre awning. That provides welcome relief both when at anchor and when under way, but is no use after sunset.
- Plenty of portholes and hatches that can be opened on both sides to provide a through draught. Sadly, it also brings in the midges!
- A wind sail above the skylight, or the forward hatch, catches every breath of air and deflects it down below.
- An automatic fan provides cooling.

However, in order to cool cabins that are too hot, real comfort throughout the boat can only be provided by an air-conditioning system. As a matter of principle, it is preferable to use a closed-circuit system, which means that the air in the cabins is continuously circulated, and in the process taken through the cooling unit of the air-conditioning system. Why closed-circuit? The introduction of outside air would mean that this air – which is hot – would constantly have to be cooled down afresh to the desired cabin temperature: a great waste of energy. It would also continuously bring in fresh moisture from outside, which would be precipitated as condensation.

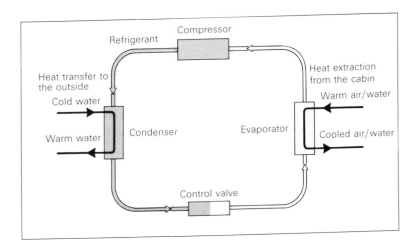

Remember: it's the exact opposite to heating which is preferably operated with outside air in order to remove moisture from the cabin. In the chapter entitled How cold is generated, the principle of cold-generation has been described in detail. There is nothing different about compartment air-conditioning. There is a similar system comprising compressor, condenser, control valve and evaporator. These components together form the refrigerant-circuit discussed previously and are usually combined into one assembly.

If air is used to move cool air around the cabin, the system is augmented by a blower, air ducts and outlet gratings. With water, the additional elements are a water pump, pipes, and a cooler/coolers with own blower.

However, there is one system in which the central evaporator is replaced by several evaporators, located in the individual cabins. The refrigerant is pumped along small-bore pipes to the individual evaporators.

The various possibilities are summarised below. Except for very small units, sea water is the only practical means of cooling the condenser. The following types of system are available:

1 Central refrigerating assembly with an evaporator positioned in the air stream of the hot air heating system, operating in the ventilating mode. This is the simplest solution if the boat already has hot air heating.

2 Central refrigerating assembly and individual conditioning units (evaporator with blower) in the cabins.

3 Central refrigerating assembly and coolers with eutectic plates and blowers in the cabins.

4 Central refrigerating assembly with blower. Air circulation via air ducts to the cabins.

5 Central refrigerating assembly with water pump. Water circulation through the cooler units in the cabins.

6 Refrigerating assembly for water circulation combined with fuelled heating unit for hot water heating. This is the boat-climate-control equipment, which provides the most comfort. Properly designed and installed, there is no requirement it won't satisfy.

It is important to establish: the necessary system output/size, drive for the compressor, cooling the condenser (air/sea water), dehumidifying the air, disposal of condensation, run of air ducts, water/refrigerant pipes.

Before we get down to detail about these points, and the different ways of providing air-conditioning, a couple more general remarks on the subject. As with heating so also with cooling: you must be quite clear from the start what it is you want. To help you decide, it is a good idea to seek the advice and support of an expert in the air-conditioning of boats. To avoid later disappointment, every boat should have its air-conditioning system individually designed and installed.

What type of boat do you have?

What size is it? Do you have a motor boat with a relatively large window area (more than 4 sq m) or a sailing boat with small portholes? How many of the windows are inclined? Is any of the glass tinted? Have all the windows got either blinds or curtains?

Are the internal furnishings light or dark? (For example: mahogany heats up to 70°C, but light-coloured furniture under the same ambient temperature conditions only heat up to 45–50°C.)

Has the hull or the superstructure got broad dark bands or large light-absorbing areas?

Have all the skylights got internal sun-blinds? Or can they have a light-coloured covering laid over the outside?

Do hatches and doors close tightly?

All this, and more, has to be taken into account when deciding on the size of an air-conditioning system. From this it follows that the first thing to do is to try to keep as much heat as possible outside the boat: heat that never gets in doesn't have to be removed by cooling.

Where is the boat being sailed?

Although in northern latitudes really hot days are pretty rare, midges can, however, become such a nuisance on sultry evenings, when anchored near a river or with a falling tide, that all external openings have to be closed tightly to keep out these pests. Down below in the cabins it then gets unpleasantly warm remarkably quickly.

If you've chosen southerly waters – such as the Mediterranean or the Caribbean – as your stamping-ground, that means real heat at least during the summer months. Even the nights don't bring much relief, since the cabins and bunks that have heated up during the day continue to radiate so much heat until long after midnight that you can't even think of going to sleep. The air-conditioning system then becomes the most prized piece of equipment on board.

What do you expect from your air-conditioning system?

Technically, installing an air-conditioning system of any output, even in boats, poses no problems – so long as the necessary electric power is available. But practically speaking, unfortunately, there are limitations on board. Since the power requirement of such a system is 10 to 20 times that of a refrigerator or a cold chest, it is necessary to consider carefully when you are going to need cooling, how much and where.

One thing you have to bear in mind is that in hot southerly waters, the cold chest or refrigerator power requirement is often enough to load the battery fully; that then leaves nothing to power the air-conditioning system. During hot weather, probably the most uncomfortable situation is when you are moored in marinas or harbours. It's sometimes inevitable, though, as you wait for friends or have repairs carried out.

This seems a suitable point to mention what temperature below deck you ought to aim for during the day – some people have got some pretty odd ideas about that. The generally accepted temperature is around 10 to 12°C below the outside temperature but no more than that.

That will no doubt surprise some people. After all, it means that for an outside temperature of 45°C a temperature below deck of 35°C is proposed. Why not a room temperature of 20°C? Because that would be too extreme a temperature contrast from a health point of view. After all, you don't spend sufficient time in the cooled cabin to enable your body to become accustomed to the low temperature; rather you're probably popping in and out of the cabin quite often.

So, an air-conditioning thermostat setting 10 to 12°C below the outside temperature is right. In harbour a low to medium refrigeration output, which one electric compressor can deliver, is sufficient for that. This will take its power from the shore connection, so that it can run for as long as you like, even through the night.

Things are rather different when you're out of harbour, for instance at anchor in a bay, without a supply from shore. Now you require a generator and you need to cool the temperature down as quickly as possible to minimise the running time of the generator. Fortunately, generators in boats as a rule have substantially more power to offer than the shore connection, so that additional compressors can be brought in to provide a powerful 'cold wave' in the evening to produce an agreeable temperature to help you get to sleep. The compressors are brought in progressively, so as not to overload the generator by taking their heavy starting currents simultaneously. In a properly designed system the generator will have no problem in supplying the running current for several compressors.

From a shore connection that would not be possible, since the standard shore nets have only 6-16 amp fuses and, furthermore, connections have to be shared by several customers.

From the above you can see how the question of how to air-condition any given boat depends, apart from the boat itself, on the individual ideas and habits of the owner. So the selection of the right unit from the vast range of air-conditioning systems on offer calls for a great deal of practical experience.

Hot air heating system used for air-conditioning

If you have a hot air heating system on board which can also be switched to 'ventilation' only, then you can insert an air cooler also fed by the cooling plant into the heating-air line. The heater switch is then set to 'ventilation', the heating system blower draws in air – preferably recirculating air, from the cabin – and the cooler cools this down before the air is returned to the cabin via the outlet.

The following diagram shows the layout:

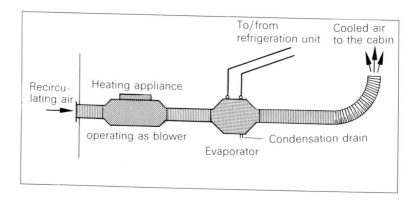

This type of compartment air-conditioning is of course only suitable for small craft. It is a practicable solution where retrofitting means that the potential for running additional air ducts/hoses is limited.

What is vital to ensure is that the cooled air enters the cabin as high up as possible. Since cold air is heavier than warm and thus sinks, it's obviously no good discharging it through low-down hot air outlets. That would just give you cold feet but do nothing to cool your head! So: extra outlets are needed for the cooled air, for example above the bench-seat. And remember to close the hot air outlets when cooling, and vice versa.

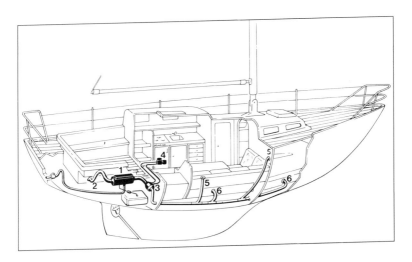

Hot air heating arranged as an air-conditioning system

1 *Heating appliance*
2 *Air intake (if possible,
    provide a connection to
    the cabin so that
    recirculated air is drawn
    in; using outside air for
    cooling is less
    advantageous for
    various reasons)*
3 *Air cooler (evaporator)*
4 *Refrigeration unit*
5 *Cold air outlet*
6 *Hot air outlet*

Air-conditioning appliances (evaporator and blower combined)

Using this type of system, the refrigerant is taken from the refrigeration installation to the appliance. That appliance is located as high up as possible in the cabin. Advantage: only the

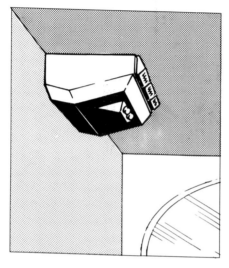

Under-deckhead appliances

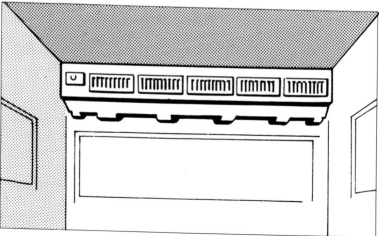

relatively small-bore pipes for the refrigerant have to be run. Disadvantage: space required in the cabin for the appliance.

This type of air-conditioning is also suitable for fitting in small boats. The appliance can be connected to the refrigeration installation already provided for the cold chest or the refrigerator (provided the output from that system is sufficient) so there is not a lot of additional expense.

Air-conditioning larger vessels or yachts, 12 m or more

For larger boats, 12 m or longer, a comprehensive approach to the design and fitting of the system is strongly recommended. If it can be fitted while the boat is being built, so much the better. No mention has been made so far of specific sizes/outputs of air-conditioning systems – for a very good reason: there are far too many individual factors to allow any generally applicable advice to be given. The best idea is to obtain and rely on expert advice when planning the installation.

Based on the summary at the beginning of the chapter, decisions must now be made between the various means of transporting cool air. The possibilities are:

- Combined evaporator and blower in the cabin
- Eutectic plate with blower
- Air cooling
- Water cooling
- Water cooling, combined with fuel-fired supplementary heating

For the condenser, the possibilities are:

- Air cooling (very rare because impractical)
- Water cooling

For the compressor the choices are:

• Mechanically driven from the main engine
• One or more electrically driven
• Combination of mechanically and electrically driven.

With so many possibilities, only a few can be gone into in detail here.

Air-conditioning with central refrigerating unit and eutectic plates with blowers

Such systems have a compressor driven by the main engine, so when the engine is running there is plenty of output available. You can see from the illustration opposite that on the drive shaft from the engine there is an electric motor in front of the compressor. This provides the drive for the compressor when connected to shore, or when there is a current supply from the boat's generator but the main engine is stopped.

The cabins have cooling units comprising an evaporator and a eutectic plate, with which you are already familiar from the cold chest. This one, naturally, is much larger.

When the main engine is running, the refrigerating compressor is connected to it via a magnetic coupling. After about half an hour, the eutectic plate has frozen into a solid block.

The trick now is, that the cooling unit is isolated and cold given off substantially, only when a built-in blower blows air over the plate. This blower is switched on/off by the cabin thermostat. So when the engine is running, a cold-reserve is built up; when it is stopped, cooling is provided without energy consumption – apart from that consumed by the blower. But adequate storage capacity means eutectic plates of appropriate size and that in turn means weight and space. So application of this system is limited to relatively large yachts.

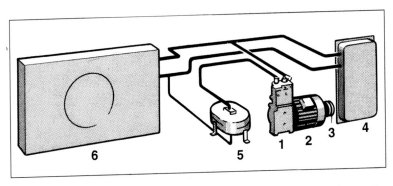

Principal components of a system with a central refrigeration unit, eutectic plates and blower.

1 *Compressor driven by main engine*
2 *Electric motor*
3 *Pulley for drive belt from engine*
4 *Eutectic plate in the refrigerator chest*
5 *Sea water cooled condenser*
6 *Cooling unit with eutectic plate and blower in the cabin*

Central air-conditioning system

This is available for operating with air or with water, and with water as a combined cooling and heating system. The cooling element (compressor, evaporator, condenser) is in one compact unit. An air cooled system additionally has a large, slow-running centrifugal blower. The air is transported via ducting of about 150 mm bore.

A water cooled system saves the space needed by this ducting, anyway 150 mm in diameter. More space can be saved by having the condenser and evaporator one inside the other.

The terms 'air' or 'water cooling system' refer to the means of transporting the heat from the cabins to the cooling unit – but the heat must then be conveyed outside. That is the job of the condenser. For installations of this size it is always (sea) water cooled. The diagram on page 100 illustrates this.

Air-conditioning the cabin

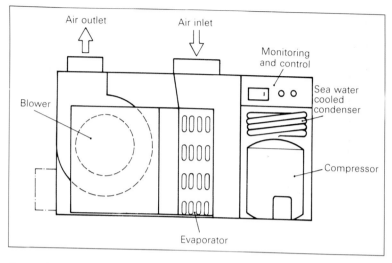

Central system for operating with cooling air

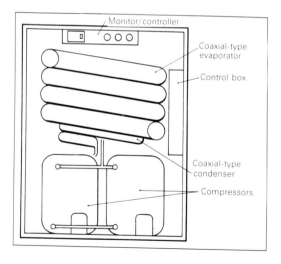

Refrigeration system for operating with cooling water

The cooling unit installed in the engine compartment of a motor yacht

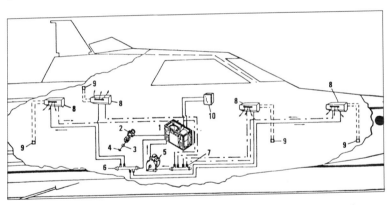

Diagram of an air-conditioning system using water cooling in a 14 m motor yacht.

1 *Refrigerating unit*
2 *Sea water pump*
3 *Strainer*
4 *Condenser cooling water inlet*
5 *Pump for water to air-conditioning appliances*

6 *Supply header*
7 *Return header*
8 *Cooling unit with blower*
9 *Thermostat*
10 *Electronic control apparatus*

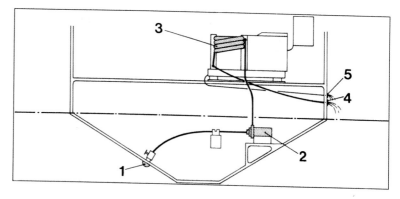

Schematic diagram of a sea water cooling system for the condenser of a boat air-conditioning system.

1 *Cooling water inlet (permanently submerged)*
2 *Water pump (salt water proof)*
3 *Condenser (sea water cooled)*
4 *Cooling water outlet*
5 *Air-conditioning system condensate drain*

Summary of features for air and water cooling

Air cooling system

Large-bore air ducts, about 150 mm dia., from cooling plant to cabins

No space required in the cabins for cooling units. Outlet grating needs no cabin space
Ducting length max. 12 m

Water cooling system

Small-bore water pipes, max. 3/4 in hose, from cooling plant to cabins

Small cooling units, with low-noise blowers, in the cabins (output 2–6 kW). Pipe length up to 20 m. Up to ten units may be connected. Individually controlled by thermostat. Glycol-water mix in the water circuit

Manufacturers of air-conditioning, heating equipment and generators

Air conditioning

Cruisair UK Ltd, 26 Old Wareham Road, Poole, Dorset BH17 7NR (0202) 716478

Condairia, Midship Boat Services Ltd, 49 Northam Road, Southampton, Hampshire SO2 0PD (0703) 331462

Krueger Ltd, Unit 16, Queensway, Stem Lane Industrial Estate, New Milton, Hampshire BH25 5NN (0425) 619869

Oceanair Marine Ltd, Atlantic House, 189 London Road, Cowplain, Hampshire PO8 8ER (0705) 269889

York International, Gardiners Lane South, Basildon, Essex SS14 3HE (0268) 287676

Heating systems and generators

Diesel and paraffin

Aqua-Marine Mfg Co UK Ltd, 216 Fair Oak Road, Bishopstoke, Eastleigh, Hampshire SO5 6NJ (0703) 694949

Blakes & Taylors, Unit 1, Newtown Business Park, Ringwood Road, Poole, Dorset BH12 3LJ (0202) 747400

Cleghorn & Waring & Co Ltd, Icknield Way, Letchwoth, Hertfordshire SG6 1EZ (0462) 480380

Eberspacher (UK) Ltd, Headlands Business Park, Salisbury Road, Ringwood, Hampshire BH24 3PB (0425) 480151

Krueger Ltd, Unit 16, Queensway, Stem Lane Industrial Estate, New Milton, Hampshire BH25 5NN (0425) 619869

Perkins Boilers Ltd, Mansfield Road, Derby, Derbyshire DE2 4BA (0332) 48235

Shipmate Stoves UK, 12 Oakdale Lodge, 131 Holdens Hill Road, Hendon, London NW4 1LH (081-959) 4203

Simpson Lawrence Ltd, 218–228 Edmiston Drive, Glasgow, Lanarkshire G51 2YT (041-427) 5331

Webasto Heating Ltd, White Rose Way, Doncaster, Carr, South Yorkshire DN4 5JH (0302) 322232

Charcoal heaters
Pascal Atkey & Son Ltd, 29–30 High Street, Cowes, Isle of Wight PO31 7RX (0983) 292381

Solid Fuel heaters
Foxton Boat Services Ltd, Bottom Lock, Foxton, Market Harborough, Leicestershire LE16 7RA (0533) 792285

LPG heaters
Kay & Co (Engineers) Ltd, Kontite Works, Moore Lane, Bolton, Lancashire BL1 4TH (0204) 21041

Calor Gas Co Ltd, Third Avenue, Millbrook Trading Estate, Southampton, Hampshire SO9 1WE (0703) 777244

Generators
Fischer Marine (UK) Ltd, The Loft, 108 Brassey Road, Winchester, Hampshire SO22 6SA (0962) 841828

G & M Power Plant Plc, Magnet Works, Whitehouse Road, Ipswich, Suffolk IP1 5LX (0473) 241000

Geko Power UK, Pixon Lane, Tavistock, Devon PL19 8DH (0822) 616060

Lister-Petter Marine (Hawker-Siddeley Power Plant Ltd), Thrupp, Stroud, Gloucestershire GL5 2BW (0453) 885166

Marine Power Bursledon, Deacons Boat Yard, Bridge Road, Bursledon, Southampton, Hampshire SO3 8AZ (0703) 403918

Tempest Diesels Ltd, Foundry Road, Stamford, Lincolnshire PE9 2RD (0780) 64387

Vetus Den Ouden Ltd, 38 South Hants Industrial Park, Totton, Southampton SO4 3SA (0703) 861033

Watermota Ltd, Abbotskerswell, Newton Abbot, Devon TQ12 5NF (0626) 333344

Index